The Hidden Language of Listening: Discovering the Secrets to Meaningful Interactions

Donovan Kian

TABLE OF CONTENT

Chapter 3: The Hidden Language of Listening   31

Nonverbal Communication: The Unsaid Messages

Understanding body language and facial expressions

Interpreting tone and intonation

Emotional Intelligence: Decoding Feelings

Recognizing and responding to emotions

Cultivating emotional awareness in listening

Chapter 4: The Secrets to Meaningful Interactions   43

Asking Effective Questions: Encouraging Dialogue

Open-ended vs. closed-ended questions

Probing for deeper understanding

Reflective Listening: Validating and Clarifying

Paraphrasing and summarizing to ensure comprehension

Reflecting on the speaker's emotions and thoughts

Chapter 5: Overcoming Listening Barriers 55

Internal Barriers: The Challenges Within

Self-centeredness and preconceived notions

Active strategies for combating internal barriers

External Barriers: The Challenges Around Us

Environmental distractions and noise

Techniques for minimizing external barriers

Chapter 6: Listening for Personal and Professional Growth 67

The Role of Listening in Personal Development

Deepening self-awareness through listening

Strengthening personal relationships

The Impact of Listening in Professional Settings

Improving teamwork and collaboration

Enhancing leadership and decision-making skills

Chapter 1: The Power of Listening

The Art of Listening: A Forgotten Skill

In today's fast-paced world, where everyone seems to be in a constant rush, the art of listening has become a forgotten skill. We live in an era of constant distractions, where our attention is divided among multiple screens and notifications. As a result, meaningful interactions have been diluted, leading to a lack of understanding, empathy, and genuine connection.

But why is being a good listener so important? The answer lies in the power of effective communication. When we truly listen to others, we create a safe space for them to express themselves, share their vulnerabilities, and be heard. This simple act of listening demonstrates respect, validation, and empathy, fostering stronger relationships and deeper connections.

Being a good listener allows us to understand others on a deeper level. By actively listening, we can pick up on subtle cues, unspoken emotions, and hidden meanings. This ability to truly hear what someone is saying goes beyond the words themselves, allowing us to grasp their true intentions and needs. It enables us to respond in a way that is meaningful and supportive, ultimately strengthening the bonds we share with others.

Moreover, the art of listening empowers us to learn and grow as individuals. When we open our ears and minds to different perspectives, we gain invaluable insights and knowledge. By actively seeking to understand others' experiences and viewpoints, we expand our own understanding of the world. This not only broadens our horizons but also facilitates personal growth, as we become more open-minded, adaptable, and compassionate individuals.

In a world filled with noise, becoming a good listener can set us apart. It allows us to stand out in a society that often values speaking over listening. By honing this forgotten skill, we can make a profound impact on the lives of others. We can be the person who makes others feel seen, heard, and valued. And in turn, we can create a ripple effect, inspiring others to become better listeners themselves.

So, let us reclaim the art of listening, for it is a skill that has the power to transform our relationships, our communities, and ultimately, our world. Let us dedicate ourselves to being present, to truly hearing others, and to embracing the beauty of meaningful interactions. By doing so, we can rediscover the hidden language of listening and unlock the secrets to a more meaningful and fulfilling life.

The significance of listening in communication

In today's fast-paced world, where everyone is constantly striving to be heard and understood, the importance of being a good listener cannot be overstated. Listening is a fundamental aspect of effective communication, and it plays a crucial role in building meaningful interactions with others. Whether you are engaging in a personal conversation, attending a business meeting, or simply interacting with colleagues and friends, being a good listener can make all the difference.

Listening is more than just hearing the words being spoken; it is about understanding the underlying message and emotions conveyed. It involves giving your full attention to the speaker, being present in the moment, and showing genuine interest in what they have to say. When you truly listen, you create a safe space for others to express themselves and share their thoughts, feelings, and experiences. This fosters a sense of trust and connection, which is vital for building strong relationships.

Moreover, being a good listener allows you to gain valuable insights and perspectives from those around you. By actively listening and seeking to understand others, you open yourself up to new ideas, different viewpoints, and alternative solutions. This not only broadens your own knowledge and understanding but also promotes a culture of collaboration and creativity.

Additionally, being a good listener enhances your ability to empathize with others. When you listen attentively, you can pick up on subtle cues, such as tone of voice, body language, and emotions, that reveal a person's true thoughts and feelings. This enables you to respond with compassion and support, deepening your connection with others and strengthening your interpersonal skills.

It is important to note that being a good listener is a skill that can be developed and refined over time. It requires practice, patience, and a genuine desire to understand others. By honing your listening skills, you can become a more effective communicator, build stronger relationships, and create a positive impact on those around you.

In conclusion, the significance of listening in communication cannot be underestimated. It is a powerful tool that allows us to connect, understand, and empathize with others. By becoming a good listener, you can enhance your communication skills, foster meaningful interactions, and build stronger relationships. So, let's strive to be better listeners and unlock the hidden language of listening for a more fulfilling and enriching life.

The effects of poor listening skills

Introduction:
In our fast-paced world filled with constant distractions and information overload, the art of listening has become undervalued. Yet, the consequences of poor listening skills are far-reaching and can negatively impact our personal and professional relationships. In this subchapter, we will explore the profound effects of poor listening skills and shed light on the importance of being a good listener.

1. Miscommunication:
When we fail to listen attentively, miscommunication becomes inevitable. Misunderstandings arise, leading to conflicts, frustration, and damaged relationships. Poor listening can result in distorted messages, missed cues, and a lack of empathy, hindering effective communication.

2. Lack of Connection:
Listening is the foundation of building strong connections with others. When we don't listen actively, we miss out on understanding others' perspectives, experiences, and emotions. Consequently, relationships become superficial, lacking depth and meaning. People may feel dismissed, unimportant, or unappreciated, which can lead to isolation and a breakdown of trust.

3. Reduced Productivity:
In various professional settings, listening skills are crucial for success. Poor listening hampers collaboration, creativity, and problem-solving abilities. Without actively listening to colleagues, clients, or superiors, important details may be overlooked, leading to errors, delays, and

missed opportunities. Moreover, poor listening can negatively impact teamwork and undermine leadership effectiveness.

4. Missed Opportunities for Learning:
Listening is not just about processing auditory information; it is about actively seeking to understand and learn from others. Poor listening prevents us from gaining new insights, perspectives, and knowledge. By failing to listen effectively, we limit our growth and miss out on valuable learning opportunities.

5. Emotional Disconnect:
Listening is an essential component of empathy and emotional intelligence. When we don't listen attentively, we fail to connect with others on an emotional level. Empathy, support, and understanding are essential for meaningful interactions. Poor listening skills can lead to emotional disconnect, leaving individuals feeling unheard and isolated.

Conclusion:
The effects of poor listening skills are far-reaching, affecting our personal relationships, professional growth, and overall well-being. By recognizing the importance of being a good listener, we can cultivate better communication, understanding, and empathy. In doing so, we unlock the power of meaningful interactions, fostering deeper connections, and creating a more harmonious and fulfilling life.

The Benefits of Being a Good Listener

In today's fast-paced world, it's easy to get caught up in our own thoughts and forget the importance of active listening. However, being a good listener can have a profound impact on our personal and professional relationships. In this subchapter, we will delve into the benefits of being a good listener and explore how it can enhance our interactions with others.

First and foremost, being a good listener shows respect and empathy towards others. When we truly listen to someone, we are giving them our undivided attention and showing that we value their thoughts and feelings. This simple act of respect can strengthen our relationships and foster a sense of trust and understanding.

Moreover, being a good listener allows us to gain valuable insights and perspectives. By actively listening to others, we open ourselves up to new ideas and experiences that we may have otherwise overlooked. This can broaden our horizons and help us become more open-minded individuals.

Additionally, being a good listener can enhance our problem-solving abilities. When we listen attentively to someone's concerns or issues, we are better equipped to offer thoughtful and relevant solutions. By understanding the full context of a situation, we can provide meaningful advice or support that can make a real difference in someone's life.

Furthermore, being a good listener can improve our communication skills. When we truly listen to others, we become more attuned to nonverbal cues, tone of voice, and underlying emotions. This heightened awareness enables us to communicate more effectively and respond appropriately to the needs of others.

Lastly, being a good listener can bring us a sense of fulfillment and satisfaction. When we take the time to listen to others and make them feel heard, we create deeper connections and foster meaningful relationships. This can lead to a greater sense of purpose and happiness in our own lives.

In conclusion, being a good listener has numerous benefits that extend beyond the act itself. It shows respect, builds trust, enhances problem-solving abilities, improves communication skills, and brings fulfillment. By cultivating the art of active listening, we can transform our interactions and lead more meaningful lives. So, let us strive to be good listeners and unlock the hidden language of meaningful interactions.

Building strong relationships

In today's fast-paced world, it is easy to get caught up in our own lives and forget the importance of building strong relationships. However, being a good listener is crucial in fostering meaningful interactions and establishing long-lasting connections with others. In this subchapter, we will explore the significance of being a good listener and how it can positively impact our relationships.

Listening is an art, and it goes beyond simply hearing the words someone is saying. It involves being fully present, paying attention to both verbal and non-verbal cues, and empathizing with the speaker. When we truly listen, we show respect and value for the other person's thoughts, feelings, and experiences. This powerful act of listening creates a safe space for open communication and trust to flourish.

One of the key aspects of being a good listener is acknowledging the importance of silence. Often, people feel compelled to fill the gaps in conversations with their own thoughts or opinions. However, by allowing moments of silence, we give the speaker the opportunity to express themselves fully without interruption. This not only shows our respect for their perspective but also encourages them to delve deeper into their thoughts and emotions.

Being a good listener also means being non-judgmental. It is essential to set aside our preconceived notions and biases, allowing the speaker to share their thoughts without fear of criticism or rejection. By suspending judgment, we create an environment that promotes open and honest dialogue, fostering understanding and empathy.

Furthermore, being an active listener involves asking thoughtful questions and providing feedback. This shows our genuine interest in the conversation and encourages the speaker to share more. By engaging in active listening, we demonstrate our commitment to the relationship and deepen our connection with others.

Building strong relationships requires effort and dedication. By honing our listening skills, we can create a solid foundation for meaningful interactions. Whether in personal or professional settings, being a good listener allows us to understand others better, resolve conflicts more effectively, and build trust and collaboration.

In conclusion, being a good listener is paramount in building strong relationships. By practicing active listening, we show respect, empathy, and understanding towards others. It is through this profound act of listening that we can foster meaningful interactions and establish deep connections with those around us. So, let us embrace the art of listening and unlock the secrets to building strong and fulfilling relationships in our lives.

Enhancing personal and professional growth

In today's fast-paced and interconnected world, the importance of being a good listener cannot be overstated. Whether in our personal relationships or professional endeavors, effective listening skills play a pivotal role in fostering meaningful interactions and unlocking our full potential.

In the subchapter "Enhancing Personal and Professional Growth" of the book "The Hidden Language of Listening: Discovering the Secrets to Meaningful Interactions," we delve into the transformative power of listening and its impact on personal and professional development. This content is addressed to everyone, regardless of their background or occupation, as the ability to listen attentively is a universal skill that can benefit individuals in all aspects of life.

Personal growth is a continuous journey, and being a good listener is a key component of this process. By actively listening to others, we gain insights into different perspectives, experiences, and emotions. This enables us to cultivate empathy, deepen connections, and broaden our understanding of the world around us. Moreover, listening attentively to ourselves can help us identify our own desires, goals, and aspirations, leading to self-discovery and personal fulfillment.

In the realm of professional growth, being a good listener is an invaluable asset. Effective communication is at the heart of successful teamwork, leadership, and customer service. By listening to colleagues, superiors, or clients, we demonstrate respect for their ideas and concerns. This not only fosters a positive work environment but also enhances collaboration and problem-solving abilities. Furthermore, active listening allows us to gather valuable feedback, identify areas for improvement, and seize opportunities for professional development.

The importance of being a good listener transcends individual relationships and has broader societal implications. It promotes inclusivity, reduces misunderstandings, and encourages open dialogue. It fosters a culture of trust, respect, and cooperation, which are crucial for building harmonious communities and organizations.

In conclusion, the subchapter "Enhancing Personal and Professional Growth" emphasizes the significance of being a good listener in our lives. By honing our listening skills and incorporating them into our personal and professional interactions, we can unlock our full potential, foster meaningful connections, and navigate the complexities of our interconnected world with empathy and understanding.

Chapter 2: The Elements of Effective Listening

Active Listening: Engaging with Intent

In today's fast-paced world, where distractions abound and time is a precious commodity, the art of active listening has become more crucial than ever before. Engaging with intent in conversations has the power to transform our interactions, deepen our relationships, and bring a new level of understanding to our lives. In this subchapter, we will explore the importance of being a good listener and delve into the secrets of active listening.

Being a good listener is not just about being physically present; it requires a conscious effort to truly engage with the speaker. It involves giving our undivided attention, demonstrating empathy, and actively participating in the conversation. When we listen actively, we signal to the other person that their words matter and that we value their thoughts and feelings.

Active listening allows us to forge deeper connections with others. By fully immersing ourselves in the conversation, we gain valuable insights and understanding. We show respect for the speaker's perspective, even if it differs from our own. By doing so, we create a safe and open space for meaningful interactions to take place.

One of the secrets to active listening lies in the skill of asking thoughtful questions. By asking open-ended questions, we encourage the speaker to share more, delve deeper into their thoughts, and express themselves fully. This not only fosters a sense of trust but also helps us to uncover hidden meanings and gain a more comprehensive understanding of the speaker's message.

Practicing active listening also allows us to become more aware of non-verbal cues. By paying attention to body language, facial expressions, and tone of voice, we can better interpret the speaker's emotions and intentions. This heightened awareness helps us to respond more effectively, offering support and encouragement where needed.

In conclusion, the importance of being a good listener cannot be overstated. Active listening involves engaging with intent, giving our full attention, and participating wholeheartedly in conversations. By actively listening, we create an environment where meaningful interactions can flourish, deepening our relationships and enhancing our understanding of others. So, let us embrace the art of active listening and unlock the hidden language that lies within every conversation.

Techniques for active listening

In today's fast-paced world, where distractions abound and communication has become increasingly digital, the importance of being a good listener cannot be overstated. Active listening is a skill that can truly transform our interactions and relationships, enabling us to connect on a deeper level with others. In this subchapter, we will explore various techniques for active listening that can help you become a better listener and enhance the meaningfulness of your interactions.

1. Pay Attention: The first and most crucial technique for active listening is to give your full attention to the speaker. Eliminate distractions, put away your phone, and maintain eye contact. By focusing your energy on the speaker, you show them that their words are important to you.

2. Empathy and Understanding: Active listening involves not only hearing the words being spoken but also understanding the emotions and perspectives behind them. Put yourself in the speaker's shoes and try to grasp their feelings and experiences. This empathetic approach allows for a deeper connection and fosters a safe space for authentic communication.

3. Reflective Listening: Reflective listening involves paraphrasing or summarizing the speaker's words to ensure that you have understood them correctly. This technique not only confirms your understanding but also shows the speaker that you are actively engaged in the conversation and value their perspective.

4. Non-Verbal Cues: Non-verbal cues, such as nodding, maintaining an open posture, and using facial expressions, can significantly enhance active listening. These cues convey your interest and encourage the speaker to continue sharing their thoughts and feelings.

5. Asking Open-Ended Questions: Asking open-ended questions not only demonstrates your active engagement but also encourages the speaker to delve deeper into their thoughts and feelings. It allows for a more meaningful conversation and helps uncover important insights.

6. Mindfulness: Practicing mindfulness can greatly enhance your ability to be an active listener. By being fully present in the moment, you can let go of distractions and truly immerse yourself in the conversation. Mindfulness enables you to pick up on subtle cues and nuances, fostering a deeper understanding of the speaker's message.

By employing these techniques for active listening, you can cultivate stronger connections, build trust, and create more meaningful interactions with others. Becoming a good listener is not only a gift to those around you but also an opportunity for personal growth and self-awareness. So, let us embark on this journey of discovery and unlock the hidden language of listening.

Overcoming distractions and barriers

In our fast-paced and technology-driven world, distractions and barriers to effective listening have become increasingly prevalent. It seems that everyone is constantly connected to their devices, multitasking, and struggling to truly engage in meaningful interactions. However, the importance of being a good listener cannot be emphasized enough. It is a vital skill that can greatly enhance our personal and professional relationships, as well as our overall well-being.

To become a good listener, we must first identify and overcome the distractions and barriers that hinder our ability to truly listen and understand others. One common distraction is the constant bombardment of information from various sources. Our smartphones, social media, and email notifications constantly vie for our attention, making it difficult to focus on the person in front of us. By consciously setting aside these distractions and giving our full attention to the speaker, we can create a space for genuine connection and understanding.

Another barrier to effective listening is our tendency to jump to conclusions or make assumptions. We often assume we know what the other person is going to say before they even finish speaking, leading to misunderstandings and missed opportunities for deeper connections. Overcoming this barrier requires us to approach each conversation with an open mind and a genuine curiosity to understand the speaker's perspective. By actively listening and asking clarifying questions, we can ensure that we are truly understanding what the other person is trying to convey.

Additionally, our own internal distractions can also hinder our ability to be present and fully engage in a conversation. Our thoughts may wander to past experiences or future concerns, preventing us from actively listening to the speaker. To overcome these internal distractions, we can practice mindfulness techniques such as deep breathing or focusing on the present moment. By consciously bringing our attention back to the conversation at hand, we can cultivate a deeper level of engagement and understanding.

Overcoming distractions and barriers to effective listening requires practice and conscious effort. However, the benefits of becoming a good listener are immeasurable. By being fully present, setting aside distractions, and approaching conversations with an open mind, we can foster meaningful interactions and create stronger connections with others. Ultimately, being a good listener not only enhances our relationships but also enriches our own lives by allowing us to truly understand and be understood. So, let us make a commitment to overcome distractions and barriers and embrace the hidden language of listening.

Empathetic Listening: Understanding Others' Perspectives

In today's fast-paced and ever-connected world, being a good listener has become a rare and valuable skill. Many of us are so caught up in our own lives and thoughts that we often forget the importance of truly understanding others. Empathetic listening is a powerful tool that can help us bridge the gap between ourselves and others, fostering meaningful interactions and deeper connections.

At its core, empathetic listening involves putting yourself in someone else's shoes and truly striving to understand their perspective. It requires setting aside your own judgments, biases, and preconceived notions, and being fully present in the moment. By doing so, you open yourself up to a whole new world of insights and understanding.

One of the key benefits of empathetic listening is that it helps build trust and rapport with others. When someone feels heard and understood, they are more likely to open up and share their thoughts and feelings. This is particularly important in personal relationships, where effective communication is the foundation for a strong and lasting bond. By practicing empathetic listening, you can create a safe space for others to express themselves and feel valued.

Empathetic listening also allows us to gain a broader and more nuanced understanding of the world around us. Each person has their own unique perspective shaped by their experiences, cultures, and beliefs. By actively seeking to understand these perspectives, we can broaden our own horizons and challenge our own biases. This not only enhances our personal growth but also helps us become more tolerant and accepting of others.

Furthermore, empathetic listening can also have a positive impact on our professional lives. In the workplace, effective communication is crucial for building strong teams and fostering collaboration. By truly understanding the perspectives of our colleagues, we can work together more efficiently and effectively. Additionally, empathetic listening can also enhance our leadership skills, as it allows us to connect with and motivate our team members on a deeper level.

In conclusion, empathetic listening is a powerful tool that can transform our interactions and relationships. By understanding others' perspectives, we not only deepen our connections but also broaden our own horizons. Whether in personal or professional settings, being a good listener is essential for creating meaningful and fulfilling interactions. So, let us embrace the power of empathetic listening and unlock the hidden language of understanding.

Developing empathy as a listener

Developing empathy as a listener is a crucial aspect of effective communication that often goes overlooked. In our fast-paced world, where everyone seems to be in a hurry to express their own thoughts and opinions, the art of truly listening has become a lost skill. However, understanding the importance of being a good listener and developing empathy can profoundly enhance our interactions with others and foster meaningful connections.

Empathy is the ability to understand and share the feelings of another person. By being empathetic listeners, we can create a safe and supportive environment for others to express themselves freely. This not only helps the speaker feel validated but also allows us to gain a deeper understanding of their thoughts, emotions, and experiences.

One key aspect of developing empathy is to set aside our own judgments and biases. Often, we tend to filter what we hear through our own preconceived notions, which can hinder our ability to truly understand the speaker's perspective. By consciously letting go of these biases, we open ourselves up to truly hearing and empathizing with the speaker.

Another important aspect of empathy as a listener is active listening. This means giving our full attention to the speaker, maintaining eye contact, and using verbal and non-verbal cues to show that we are engaged in the conversation. Active listening also involves asking open-ended questions and paraphrasing what the speaker has said to ensure that we have understood them correctly.

Developing empathy as a listener also requires us to practice patience and compassion. It is important to remember that everyone has their own unique experiences and emotions. By being patient and compassionate, we create a safe space for others to share their vulnerabilities without fear of judgment or dismissal.

Furthermore, empathy allows us to connect on a deeper level with those around us. It helps build trust and strengthens relationships. When we genuinely listen and empathize with others, we demonstrate that we value their thoughts and emotions, which in turn encourages them to open up and share more.

In conclusion, developing empathy as a listener is a powerful tool that can transform our interactions with others. By setting aside our own biases, actively listening, practicing patience, and showing compassion, we can create a space where meaningful connections can flourish. The importance of being a good listener cannot be overstated, as it not only benefits the speaker but also enhances our own understanding of the world around us. Let us strive to develop empathy as listeners and unlock the hidden language of meaningful interactions.

Creating a safe and supportive environment

In the hustle and bustle of our daily lives, it can be easy to overlook the importance of being a good listener. Yet, the ability to truly listen and understand others is a skill that can transform our interactions and relationships. In this subchapter, we will delve into the significance of creating a safe and supportive environment for effective listening.

Listening is not merely a passive act of hearing someone's words. It goes beyond that; it involves being fully present and engaged in the conversation. By creating a safe and supportive environment, we allow others to express themselves freely, knowing that their thoughts and feelings will be acknowledged and respected.

First and foremost, one must cultivate a non-judgmental mindset. It is essential to suspend our own biases, opinions, and preconceived notions, allowing the speaker to feel comfortable sharing their experiences. By doing so, we show that we genuinely value their perspective and are willing to understand their point of view.

Active listening techniques play a crucial role in fostering a safe environment. This involves maintaining eye contact, nodding to indicate understanding, and providing verbal cues such as "I see," "I understand," or "Tell me more." By actively demonstrating our engagement, we encourage the speaker to open up and share more deeply.

Another aspect of creating a safe and supportive environment is practicing empathy. Empathy involves not only understanding someone's emotions but also sharing in those feelings. By putting ourselves in the speaker's shoes, we can better relate to their experiences, validating their emotions, and fostering a deeper connection.

A safe and supportive environment also requires confidentiality. When someone confides in us, it is crucial to respect their trust and keep their information confidential. This builds a sense of security and encourages open and honest communication.

Lastly, creating a safe and supportive environment requires patience and understanding. It is essential to give the speaker ample time to express themselves fully without interruption or judgment. By allowing them to speak uninterrupted, we demonstrate that we value their thoughts and opinions.

In conclusion, creating a safe and supportive environment is a fundamental aspect of being a good listener. By cultivating a non-judgmental mindset, practicing active listening, empathy, confidentiality, and patience, we can foster an environment where meaningful interactions thrive. In doing so, we create a space where individuals feel heard, validated, and respected, leading to stronger connections and deeper understanding in all our relationships.

Chapter 3: The Hidden Language of Listening

Nonverbal Communication: The Unsaid Messages

In our daily lives, we often focus on the words being spoken during a conversation. However, what we fail to realize is that there is another language being communicated simultaneously – the language of nonverbal cues. Nonverbal communication plays a vital role in our interactions, often conveying messages that words alone cannot express. Understanding this hidden language is the key to becoming a more effective and empathetic listener.

Nonverbal cues include facial expressions, body language, tone of voice, and even the space between individuals during a conversation. These cues provide valuable insights into a person's emotions, intentions, and overall state of being. While words may be carefully chosen, nonverbal cues are often involuntary and give us glimpses into a person's true thoughts and feelings.

Being aware of nonverbal communication is especially important because it allows us to fully grasp the meaning behind someone's words. For instance, a person may say they are fine, but their slouched posture, frowning face, and lack of eye contact reveal their true distress. By paying attention to these unsaid messages, we can respond with empathy and offer the support that is truly needed.

Nonverbal communication also helps us gauge the level of engagement and interest in a conversation. For instance, crossed arms, tapping feet, or a distracted gaze can indicate boredom or disinterest. On the other hand, open body language, nodding, and maintaining eye contact show active listening and genuine engagement. By understanding these cues, we can adjust our own behavior to create a more meaningful and engaging interaction.

Moreover, nonverbal communication is particularly relevant in situations where language barriers exist, such as intercultural interactions. In such cases, relying solely on words can lead to misunderstandings and misinterpretations. Nonverbal cues, however, are universal and can bridge the gap between languages, helping us connect on a deeper level.

In conclusion, nonverbal communication is the unsung hero of meaningful interactions. By paying attention to the unsaid messages conveyed through nonverbal cues, we can gain a deeper understanding of others and create more impactful connections. Whether it is in personal relationships, professional settings, or even casual conversations, being attuned to this hidden language will undoubtedly enhance our ability to be good listeners. So, let us not only listen with our ears but also with our eyes and hearts, as we uncover the secrets of nonverbal communication.

Understanding body language and facial expressions

Understanding body language and facial expressions is a crucial aspect of effective communication. In the book "The Hidden Language of Listening: Discovering the Secrets to Meaningful Interactions," we delve into the significance of decoding these non-verbal cues to become better listeners. Whether you are a student, a professional, or simply someone interested in improving their communication skills, this subchapter will provide you with valuable insights into the importance of understanding body language and facial expressions.

Body language and facial expressions often reveal more about a person's thoughts and feelings than their words do. By paying attention to these non-verbal cues, we can gain a deeper understanding of the speaker's true intentions and emotions. This enables us to respond more effectively, fostering meaningful interactions and building stronger relationships.

For example, a clenched jaw or furrowed brows can indicate a person's anxiety or frustration. By recognizing these signs, we can approach the conversation with empathy and understanding, offering support or assistance if needed. On the other hand, open and relaxed body language can signify comfort and trust, creating a safe space for open dialogue.

Understanding body language and facial expressions also helps us identify underlying emotions that may not be explicitly expressed. A smile can indicate happiness, but it can also mask sadness or insecurity. By being attuned to these subtleties, we can offer the appropriate support or encouragement, ensuring that our interactions are meaningful and impactful.

Additionally, body language and facial expressions play a crucial role in building rapport and establishing trust. Maintaining eye contact, nodding affirmatively, and mirroring the speaker's gestures can all contribute to creating a positive connection. Conversely, crossed arms, averted gaze, or fidgeting can indicate disinterest or discomfort. Recognizing these signals allows us to adjust our own behavior to foster a more engaging and inclusive conversation.

In conclusion, understanding body language and facial expressions is an essential skill for effective listening and meaningful interactions. By honing this skill, we can decode the hidden language behind non-verbal cues, gaining a deeper understanding of others and fostering stronger connections. Whether in personal or professional settings, this knowledge will empower you to become a better listener and communicator, enhancing the quality of your relationships and interactions.

Interpreting tone and intonation

In our daily lives, we engage in countless conversations, both verbal and nonverbal. However, have you ever stopped to consider the impact of tone and intonation in these interactions? The way we speak and the subtle nuances of our tone can greatly influence the meaning and effectiveness of our communication. In this subchapter, we will delve into the significance of interpreting tone and intonation, and how being attuned to these elements can enhance our communication skills.

Tone refers to the quality or character of our voice, while intonation refers to the rise and fall of our pitch when we speak. Together, they create a powerful tool for conveying emotions, emphasizing certain words or phrases, and establishing rapport with others. By understanding and interpreting tone and intonation, we can develop a deeper level of empathy, improve our listening skills, and foster more meaningful interactions.

When we listen to someone speak, we often focus on the words they are saying, but it is equally important to pay attention to the tone and intonation behind those words. For instance, a simple statement like "I'm fine" can have vastly different meanings depending on the tone and intonation used. It could be a genuine expression of contentment, or it could be a subtle indication of sadness or frustration. By tuning in to these vocal cues, we can better comprehend the speaker's true emotions and respond accordingly.

Additionally, understanding tone and intonation can help us become better listeners. By picking up on the subtle shifts in someone's tone, we can identify when they are becoming excited, agitated, or disinterested. This awareness allows us to adapt our own communication style, showing empathy and support when needed or adjusting our approach for a more engaging conversation.

In conclusion, understanding and interpreting tone and intonation is key to becoming a skilled communicator and listener. By paying attention to these vocal cues, we can uncover the hidden meanings behind words, build stronger connections with others, and create more meaningful interactions. So, let us embark on this journey of discovering the secrets of tone and intonation, and unlock the hidden language of listening for more fulfilling relationships.

Emotional Intelligence: Decoding Feelings

In our fast-paced world, where communication has become increasingly digital, the art of listening is often overlooked. Yet, being a good listener is a skill that holds immense importance in our personal and professional lives. It is through listening that we can truly understand others, connect on a deeper level, and build meaningful relationships. This subchapter, "Emotional Intelligence: Decoding Feelings," delves into the vital role emotional intelligence plays in effective listening.

Emotional intelligence refers to the ability to recognize, understand, and manage our own emotions, as well as those of others. It is the key to decoding feelings and gaining valuable insights into the unspoken messages behind words. By developing emotional intelligence, we can enhance our listening skills and create a safe and supportive environment for open communication.

When we listen with emotional intelligence, we go beyond merely hearing the words being spoken. We pay attention to the speaker's tone of voice, body language, and subtle cues that reveal their true emotions. By doing so, we are better equipped to empathize with their feelings, validate their experiences, and respond appropriately.

Decoding feelings requires a high level of self-awareness and empathy. It involves putting ourselves in the speaker's shoes and striving to understand their perspective without judgment. This subchapter provides practical techniques and exercises to cultivate emotional intelligence, such as active listening, non-verbal communication analysis, and reflecting on our own emotional responses.

By becoming skilled at decoding feelings, we can navigate through difficult conversations and resolve conflicts more effectively. We can also build trust, foster mutual respect, and create a sense of belonging in our interactions with others. Emotional intelligence allows us to connect with people on a deeper level, forging meaningful relationships that enhance our personal and professional lives.

Whether you are a student, a parent, a friend, or a professional, the importance of being a good listener cannot be underestimated. In this subchapter, "Emotional Intelligence: Decoding Feelings," you will discover the secrets to meaningful interactions through the lens of emotional intelligence. By learning to decode feelings, you will not only improve your listening skills but also enhance your ability to connect with others and create a positive impact in the world around you.

So, join us on this transformative journey as we unlock the hidden language of listening and embrace the power of emotional intelligence in every aspect of our lives.

Recognizing and responding to emotions

In the realm of human communication, emotions play a vital role in understanding and connecting with others. Being able to recognize and respond to emotions is a fundamental aspect of being a good listener. In this subchapter, we will delve into the importance of recognizing and responding to emotions, and how it can enhance our interactions and relationships with others.

Emotions are an inherent part of the human experience. They shape our perceptions, guide our actions, and dictate our responses to various situations. When we can recognize and understand the emotions expressed by others, we gain a deeper insight into their thoughts, feelings, and needs. This understanding allows us to respond in a way that is empathetic, supportive, and meaningful.

Recognizing emotions involves paying attention to both verbal and non-verbal cues. While words can provide some insight into how someone is feeling, non-verbal cues such as facial expressions, body language, and tone of voice often reveal a person's true emotional state. By actively observing these cues, we can gain a more accurate understanding of what someone is trying to communicate.

Once we have recognized the emotions being expressed, responding appropriately is crucial. This involves validating the person's feelings and providing a safe space for them to express themselves. Responding to emotions requires active listening, empathy, and the ability to withhold judgment. By doing so, we create an environment that fosters trust, understanding, and open communication.

Recognizing and responding to emotions is not only important in personal relationships but also in professional settings. In the workplace, understanding the emotions of colleagues, clients, and superiors can improve teamwork, productivity, and overall job satisfaction. It enables us to offer support, address conflicts, and provide effective feedback.

In conclusion, recognizing and responding to emotions is an essential skill for everyone. It allows us to connect on a deeper level with others, fostering stronger relationships and meaningful interactions. By paying attention to verbal and non-verbal cues, validating emotions, and providing a safe space for expression, we can create an environment where people feel heard, understood, and valued. Whether in personal or professional settings, mastering this skill will undoubtedly enhance our ability to be effective listeners and communicators.

Cultivating emotional awareness in listening

In our fast-paced, technology-driven world, it can be easy to forget the importance of being a good listener. We are constantly bombarded with information and distractions, making it challenging to truly connect with others in a meaningful way. However, the ability to listen actively and empathetically is crucial for building strong relationships and fostering understanding.

One key aspect of becoming a better listener is cultivating emotional awareness. Emotional awareness involves being attuned to both our own emotions and those of others. It requires us to be present in the moment and fully engaged in the conversation. By developing this skill, we can create a safe and supportive environment for open communication.

When we are emotionally aware in listening, we are able to pick up on subtle cues and non-verbal communication, such as body language and tone of voice. These cues often reveal the true emotions behind the words being spoken. By recognizing and acknowledging these emotions, we can respond in a more genuine and empathetic manner, deepening the level of understanding between ourselves and the speaker.

Emotional awareness also allows us to better regulate our own emotions during a conversation. We can become more conscious of how our own feelings may be influencing our listening and responding. For example, if we are feeling defensive or impatient, we may not be fully present in the conversation, hindering our ability to listen effectively. By being aware of our emotions, we can take steps to manage them, ensuring that we are truly attentive and receptive to what is being said.

To cultivate emotional awareness in listening, it is essential to practice mindfulness. Mindfulness involves being fully present in the moment, without judgment or distraction. By practicing mindfulness regularly, we can develop the ability to tune in to our own emotions and the emotions of others, enhancing our listening skills.

In conclusion, cultivating emotional awareness in listening is a vital skill for meaningful interactions. By being emotionally aware, we can better understand the emotions behind the words, create a supportive environment for communication, and regulate our own emotions for more effective listening. So, let us strive to be present, empathetic, and mindful listeners, as these qualities are the foundation for building strong and meaningful relationships with others.

Chapter 4: The Secrets to Meaningful Interactions

Asking Effective Questions: Encouraging Dialogue

In today's fast-paced world, effective communication is more important than ever. Whether it's in personal relationships, professional settings, or even casual conversations, the ability to actively listen and engage in meaningful dialogue is a skill that can greatly enhance our interactions. This subchapter, titled "Asking Effective Questions: Encouraging Dialogue," from the book "The Hidden Language of Listening: Discovering the Secrets to Meaningful Interactions," is geared towards everyone who recognizes the importance of being a good listener and wishes to improve their communication skills.

Being a good listener goes beyond simply hearing what others say; it involves actively participating in the conversation, understanding the speaker's perspective, and asking thoughtful questions that encourage dialogue. The art of asking effective questions is a powerful tool that can foster deeper connections, promote understanding, and facilitate problem-solving.

This subchapter delves into the significance of asking the right questions and explores various strategies to enhance our questioning skills. It emphasizes the importance of open-ended questions that invite detailed responses and avoid simple "yes" or "no" answers. By using open-ended questions, we create opportunities for others to express their thoughts, feelings, and experiences more freely, enabling a richer and more meaningful conversation.

Additionally, this subchapter highlights the role of active listening in formulating effective questions. It provides practical tips on how to listen attentively, show genuine interest, and use verbal and non-verbal cues to encourage others to share more. By demonstrating our commitment to understanding and empathizing with the speaker, we create a safe and supportive environment that encourages open dialogue.

Furthermore, the subchapter addresses common pitfalls to avoid when asking questions, such as leading or judgmental questions that may hinder open communication. It helps readers recognize the potential impact of poorly framed questions and offers alternative approaches to ensure productive and respectful conversations.

Ultimately, the subchapter aims to empower readers with the skills and knowledge needed to become effective questioners, fostering dialogue and promoting meaningful interactions. By mastering the art of asking effective questions, we can transform our conversations, deepen our connections, and build stronger relationships in all areas of our lives.

Open-ended vs. closed-ended questions

In the realm of effective communication and meaningful interactions, the way we ask questions plays a crucial role. Questions can either open up the conversation and invite deeper exploration or limit it to a specific response. Understanding the distinction between open-ended and closed-ended questions is key to becoming a good listener and fostering more meaningful connections with others.

Open-ended questions are those that encourage the recipient to share their thoughts, feelings, and experiences in a more detailed and expansive manner. These questions cannot be answered with a simple "yes" or "no" and instead require the person to reflect and provide a more thoughtful response. They allow for a broader range of possibilities and offer the opportunity to delve deeper into a topic. Examples of open-ended questions include "What are your thoughts on this?" or "How did that experience make you feel?"

Closed-ended questions, on the other hand, typically limit the response to a specific answer or a short piece of information. They are designed to obtain a specific piece of information, often requiring a simple "yes" or "no" response. While closed-ended questions can be useful in certain situations, such as when seeking clarification or specific details, they can also hinder the development of a meaningful conversation. Examples of closed-ended questions include "Did you enjoy the movie?" or "Have you finished the report yet?"

By using open-ended questions, we demonstrate a genuine interest in the other person's thoughts and experiences. These types of questions encourage active listening and provide space for the speaker to express themselves fully. Open-ended questions also allow for a deeper exploration of topics, fostering a sense of trust and understanding between individuals. As a result, relationships are strengthened, and connections are made on a more profound level.

Being aware of the impact our questioning style has on conversations is an essential aspect of becoming a good listener. By consciously incorporating open-ended questions into our interactions, we create an environment where others feel valued and heard. We are able to gain deeper insights into their perspectives and experiences, ultimately leading to more meaningful and fulfilling interactions.

In conclusion, understanding the distinction between open-ended and closed-ended questions is crucial to becoming a good listener and enhancing the quality of our interactions. By utilizing open-ended questions, we create space for others to share their thoughts and feelings, fostering a deeper connection and understanding. So, let us embrace the power of open-ended questions and unlock the hidden language of listening for more meaningful interactions with everyone we encounter.

Probing for deeper understanding

In our fast-paced world, where communication often feels shallow and surface-level, the importance of being a good listener cannot be overstated. The power of listening goes beyond hearing words; it lies in our ability to truly understand and connect with others on a deeper level. In this subchapter, "Probing for Deeper Understanding," we delve into the secrets of meaningful interactions and how to unlock the hidden language of listening.

When we engage in conversations, it is easy to get caught up in our own thoughts and opinions, often missing the true essence of what the other person is trying to convey. However, by mastering the art of probing for deeper understanding, we can unlock a wealth of knowledge, emotions, and perspectives that can enrich our relationships and expand our own personal growth.

Probing is about asking the right questions at the right time. It involves a genuine curiosity and a willingness to delve beneath the surface. By asking open-ended questions that invite the speaker to share their thoughts, feelings, and experiences, we create an environment of trust and vulnerability. This allows us to go beyond superficial conversations and explore the depths of someone's story.

One of the essential skills of probing is active listening. It requires our full attention and an open mind. We need to be fully present, not just physically, but also mentally and emotionally. By suspending judgment and truly empathizing with the speaker, we can create a safe space for them to open up and share their truth.

Probing for deeper understanding also involves reading between the lines. It is about paying attention to non-verbal cues, such as body language and tone of voice. Sometimes, what is left unsaid holds more weight than the words themselves. By picking up on these subtle signals, we can ask targeted questions that lead to a deeper exploration of the speaker's thoughts and emotions.

As we become adept at probing for deeper understanding, we unlock the secrets to meaningful interactions. We develop stronger relationships, foster empathy, and gain valuable insights into ourselves and others. This skill allows us to bridge gaps, resolve conflicts, and build a more harmonious world.

In conclusion, the importance of being a good listener cannot be underestimated. By mastering the art of probing for deeper understanding, we can unlock the hidden language of listening and discover the secrets to meaningful interactions. Whether in our personal or professional lives, the ability to truly understand and connect with others on a deeper level is a skill that can transform our relationships and enrich our lives. So, let us embrace the power of probing and embark on a journey of authentic connections and profound understanding.

Reflective Listening: Validating and Clarifying

In our fast-paced world, where distractions are abundant and attention spans are decreasing, the importance of being a good listener cannot be overstated. Whether you are engaging in a conversation with a loved one, a colleague, or a stranger, truly listening can have a profound impact on the quality of your interactions and the depth of your relationships. This subchapter will explore the concept of reflective listening, focusing specifically on the techniques of validating and clarifying.

Reflective listening goes beyond simply hearing the words being spoken; it involves actively paying attention to the speaker's message, emotions, and intentions. Validating is one of the fundamental components of reflective listening. When we validate someone, we acknowledge their feelings and experiences, letting them know that we understand and accept their perspective. This validation creates an environment of trust and empathy, which encourages open and honest communication.

To validate effectively, it is crucial to practice empathy and put yourself in the speaker's shoes. By acknowledging their emotions and experiences, you are showing them that their thoughts and feelings are valid and worthy of consideration. This validation can be as simple as saying, "I understand how you feel" or "That must have been challenging for you." Such statements demonstrate your genuine interest in their words and experiences.

Another essential aspect of reflective listening is clarifying. Oftentimes, miscommunication arises from misunderstandings or assumptions. By seeking clarification, you ensure that you have a comprehensive understanding of the speaker's message. This can be done by paraphrasing or summarizing their words and asking open-ended questions. These clarifying techniques not only show your commitment to understanding but also allow the speaker to correct any misconceptions or provide further explanation.

Reflective listening, through validation and clarification, allows for deeper connections and meaningful interactions. It cultivates an environment where individuals feel heard, respected, and valued. By honing your skills as a reflective listener, you can enhance your personal relationships, improve your professional collaborations, and foster a greater sense of understanding in all areas of your life.

In conclusion, being a good listener is not just a passive act; it requires active engagement and a willingness to validate and clarify. The importance of reflective listening cannot be overstated in today's society. By validating the experiences and emotions of others, and seeking clarification when needed, you can create an environment of trust, empathy, and understanding. So, let us strive to become better listeners and unlock the hidden language of meaningful interactions.

Paraphrasing and summarizing to ensure comprehension

Paraphrasing and summarizing are two crucial techniques that can greatly enhance comprehension during conversations. In the realm of effective listening, these skills play a vital role in ensuring a meaningful interaction between individuals. Whether you are engaged in a personal conversation, professional setting, or any other social context, the ability to paraphrase and summarize accurately demonstrates your commitment to understanding others.

Paraphrasing involves restating someone's words or ideas in your own words, capturing the essence of their message. This technique not only confirms your comprehension but also allows the speaker to clarify any misunderstanding. When you paraphrase, you demonstrate active listening and genuine interest in the speaker's perspective. By rephrasing their thoughts, you can also help them gain new insights into their own ideas. This process promotes a deeper connection and enables a more profound exchange of thoughts and emotions.

Summarizing, on the other hand, involves condensing the main points or ideas expressed by the speaker. It provides a concise overview of the conversation, allowing both parties to assess their understanding of the topic. Summaries help identify any gaps in comprehension and provide an opportunity for further clarification. By summarizing effectively, you exhibit your grasp of the key elements of the conversation and facilitate a more efficient and focused discussion.

For effective paraphrasing and summarizing, it is essential to listen attentively, paying close attention to both verbal and non-verbal cues. Active listening involves fully engaging with the speaker, avoiding distractions, and maintaining eye contact. It is also crucial to ask clarifying questions when necessary, ensuring that you comprehend the speaker's intended meaning.

By paraphrasing and summarizing, you not only enhance your own comprehension but also contribute to the overall quality of the conversation. These techniques foster empathy, respect, and understanding between individuals. They enable a deeper connection and facilitate meaningful interactions.

In conclusion, paraphrasing and summarizing are indispensable tools for effective listening. By employing these techniques, you exhibit your commitment to understanding others and contribute to the overall quality of conversations. Whether in personal or professional settings, the ability to paraphrase and summarize accurately ensures comprehension, deepens connections, and promotes meaningful interactions.

Reflecting on the speaker's emotions and thoughts

In our fast-paced world, it is becoming increasingly difficult to truly connect with others on a deep level. We often find ourselves half-listening, with our minds preoccupied by our own thoughts and concerns. However, being a good listener is not just about hearing the words someone is saying—it is about understanding their emotions and thoughts behind those words. This subchapter will delve into the importance of reflecting on the speaker's emotions and thoughts, and how it can lead to more meaningful interactions.

When we reflect on the speaker's emotions, we go beyond the surface level and try to understand what they are feeling. Is the speaker happy, sad, frustrated, or excited? By paying attention to their emotional cues, we can empathize with their experiences and provide the support they need. It is crucial to remember that emotions are a vital part of communication, and by acknowledging and validating them, we create a safe space for others to express themselves.

Additionally, reflecting on the speaker's thoughts allows us to delve deeper into their perspectives and understand their point of view. This means actively listening to their ideas, opinions, and beliefs without judgment. By doing so, we can challenge our own biases and broaden our horizons. Realizing that everyone's thoughts are valid and important fosters a sense of respect and acceptance, leading to more harmonious and inclusive conversations.

Reflecting on both emotions and thoughts requires active engagement in the conversation. It means being fully present, setting aside our own concerns, and genuinely trying to understand the speaker's experience.

This level of attentiveness not only strengthens our relationships but also allows us to gain insights and knowledge that we might have missed otherwise.

Being a good listener is a skill that can be developed with practice, and it holds enormous significance in our personal and professional lives. By reflecting on the speaker's emotions and thoughts, we can create deeper connections, build trust, and foster a sense of belonging. It is through meaningful interactions that we can truly understand and appreciate the hidden language of listening.

In conclusion, the subchapter "Reflecting on the Speaker's Emotions and Thoughts" emphasizes the importance of going beyond surface-level listening. By actively engaging with the speaker's emotions and thoughts, we can create meaningful interactions that lead to stronger relationships and a deeper understanding of others. Whether in personal or professional settings, being a good listener is a powerful tool that allows us to connect with others on a profound level. So let us embrace the hidden language of listening and unlock the secrets to more meaningful interactions.

Chapter 5: Overcoming Listening Barriers

Internal Barriers: The Challenges Within

In our journey towards becoming better listeners, we often focus on external factors such as distractions, noise, or the speaker's communication skills. However, it is equally important to recognize and address the internal barriers that hinder our ability to truly listen and engage with others. These internal barriers, rooted in our thoughts, emotions, and biases, can be the biggest challenge we face in meaningful interactions.

One of the most significant internal barriers to effective listening is our own preoccupation with ourselves. We often get caught up in our own thoughts, worries, or judgments, making it difficult to fully focus on what the speaker is saying. Our mind may wander, and we may start formulating responses even before the speaker has finished. This self-centeredness inhibits our ability to truly understand the speaker's perspective and limits our capacity to empathize.

Another internal barrier we encounter is the influence of our emotions. Our emotional state can significantly impact our listening skills. When we are feeling stressed, angry, or overwhelmed, we may become defensive, dismissive, or impatient. These emotions cloud our ability to listen with an open mind and empathetic heart. Recognizing and managing our emotions is crucial for creating a safe and conducive environment for meaningful conversations.

Furthermore, our biases and assumptions can act as formidable internal barriers to effective listening. We all have inherent biases based on our experiences, beliefs, and cultural backgrounds. These biases can lead to snap judgments or assumptions about others, preventing us from truly hearing their words and understanding their perspectives. Overcoming these biases requires a conscious effort to suspend judgment, cultivate curiosity, and approach every conversation with an open mind.

Addressing these internal barriers and becoming a better listener requires self-awareness, mindfulness, and practice. It demands that we shift our focus from ourselves to the speaker, actively engage with their words, and suspend our judgments and preconceived notions. By doing so, we create a space for authentic connections, mutual understanding, and meaningful interactions.

Ultimately, being a good listener is not just about acquiring the right techniques or skills; it is a mindset, a way of being in the world. It is about genuinely valuing and respecting others' perspectives, honoring their experiences, and creating a safe space for their voices to be heard. By recognizing and overcoming our internal barriers, we can unlock the hidden language of listening and embark on a transformative journey towards deeper connections and more meaningful interactions with everyone we encounter.

Self-centeredness and preconceived notions

In our fast-paced and interconnected world, it is all too easy to become self-centered and hold preconceived notions about others. These tendencies can hinder our ability to engage in meaningful interactions and truly listen to those around us. In this subchapter, we will explore the detrimental effects of self-centeredness and preconceived notions, as well as the importance of overcoming these barriers to become better listeners.

Self-centeredness is a natural human inclination, rooted in our instinct for self-preservation and survival. However, when this self-focus becomes excessive, it can lead to a lack of empathy and understanding towards others. We may find ourselves constantly thinking about our own needs, desires, and opinions, leaving little room for the perspectives and experiences of those we interact with. This self-centeredness creates a barrier between us and others, preventing us from truly listening and connecting with them.

Similarly, preconceived notions can cloud our judgment and prevent us from seeing others for who they truly are. We often form these notions based on stereotypes, biases, or past experiences, which can lead to unfair judgments and misunderstandings. When we approach conversations with preconceived notions, we are not open to new information or different perspectives. This closed-mindedness hinders our ability to listen attentively and engage in meaningful dialogue.

Being a good listener requires us to step outside of our own self-centeredness and let go of our preconceived notions. It involves actively paying attention to the speaker, seeking to understand their thoughts, feelings, and motivations. By doing so, we can foster a sense of empathy and connection, allowing for more meaningful interactions.

Understanding the importance of being a good listener goes beyond the basic act of hearing. It is about acknowledging the value and worth of every individual's voice and experiences. When we truly listen, we create a safe space for others to share their thoughts and feelings, fostering trust and deepening our relationships.

Overcoming self-centeredness and preconceived notions requires self-reflection and a willingness to challenge our own beliefs. It involves recognizing that our perspectives are not the only valid ones and being open to learning from others. By actively working to become better listeners, we can break down barriers, foster understanding, and create a more inclusive and compassionate world.

In the upcoming chapters, we will delve deeper into the strategies and techniques for becoming a good listener and overcoming self-centeredness and preconceived notions. By embracing these principles, we can unlock the hidden language of listening and discover the secrets to more meaningful interactions.

Active strategies for combating internal barriers

Becoming a good listener is a skill that can greatly enhance our relationships, both personal and professional. However, there are often internal barriers that prevent us from fully engaging in meaningful interactions. These barriers can include distractions, preconceived notions, and our own internal chatter. In this subchapter, we will explore active strategies for combating these internal barriers and becoming better listeners.

One effective strategy is to practice mindfulness. Mindfulness involves being fully present in the moment, without judgment or distraction. By practicing mindfulness, we can train our minds to focus on the speaker and their message, rather than allowing our thoughts to wander. This can be achieved through techniques such as deep breathing, meditation, or simply paying attention to our surroundings.

Another strategy is to suspend our assumptions and preconceived notions. Often, we enter conversations with preconceived ideas about the speaker or the topic at hand. This can prevent us from truly listening and understanding the other person's perspective. By consciously setting aside our assumptions and approaching each conversation with an open mind, we can create space for genuine understanding and connection.

It is also important to manage our internal chatter. Our minds are constantly bombarded with thoughts, judgments, and distractions. This internal chatter can make it difficult to truly listen to others. One way to combat this is by practicing active listening techniques, such as paraphrasing or summarizing what the speaker has said. This not only helps us stay engaged, but also shows the speaker that we are actively listening and interested in what they have to say.

In addition, adopting a growth mindset can greatly enhance our listening skills. A growth mindset is the belief that our abilities and intelligence can be developed through dedication and hard work. By embracing a growth mindset, we can approach conversations as opportunities for learning and growth, rather than feeling the need to prove ourselves or be right. This mindset encourages us to ask questions, seek clarification, and genuinely engage with the speaker.

In conclusion, becoming a good listener requires actively combating internal barriers. By practicing mindfulness, suspending assumptions, managing internal chatter, and adopting a growth mindset, we can enhance our listening skills and create more meaningful interactions. These strategies are applicable to everyone, regardless of their background or profession. So, let's all strive to become better listeners and cultivate deeper connections with those around us.

External Barriers: The Challenges Around Us

In our quest for meaningful interactions, it is essential to recognize the external barriers that can hinder effective listening. These challenges, present in our surroundings, can often go unnoticed but have a significant impact on our ability to truly connect with others. Understanding and overcoming these external barriers is crucial if we want to become better listeners and foster genuine relationships.

One of the most common external barriers is noise pollution. In today's fast-paced world, we are constantly bombarded with noise from various sources, such as traffic, technology, and crowded spaces. This excessive noise can make it difficult to focus on what others are saying, leading to miscommunication and misunderstandings. To overcome this challenge, we need to create quiet environments whenever possible, where both the speaker and listener can fully engage in the conversation without distractions.

Another external barrier that hinders effective listening is the digital age. With the rise of smartphones and social media, we are constantly connected to our devices, often at the expense of real-life interactions. The temptation to check notifications or respond to messages can divert our attention away from the person in front of us. It is crucial to set boundaries and prioritize face-to-face conversations, ensuring that we are fully present and engaged with those around us.

Cultural differences can also pose challenges to meaningful interactions. Each culture has its own communication norms and styles, which can lead to misunderstandings if not acknowledged and respected. By educating ourselves about different cultural practices and being open-minded, we can bridge these gaps and create an inclusive environment for effective listening.

Furthermore, external distractions like visual stimuli or environmental factors can also impede our ability to listen attentively. A cluttered or uncomfortable space can make it challenging to focus, while visual distractions can divert our attention away from the speaker. Creating a conducive environment for listening, free from distractions, is crucial for fostering meaningful interactions.

In conclusion, external barriers pose significant challenges to effective listening. Noise pollution, the digital age, cultural differences, and distractions all play a role in hindering our ability to connect with others. Recognizing and addressing these barriers is essential if we want to become better listeners and cultivate meaningful relationships. By creating quiet spaces, setting boundaries with technology, respecting cultural differences, and removing distractions, we can overcome these challenges and unlock the hidden language of listening.

Environmental distractions and noise

Environmental distractions and noise play a significant role in our ability to be good listeners. In today's fast-paced world, it is becoming increasingly difficult to find a quiet and peaceful space where we can truly focus on listening to others. This subchapter explores the impact of environmental distractions and noise on our listening skills and offers strategies to overcome these challenges.

In our modern society, we are constantly bombarded with various types of distractions. Whether it is the constant buzzing of our smartphones, the chatter of people around us, or the blaring horns of traffic, these distractions make it hard for us to concentrate on what someone is saying. As a result, our ability to actively listen and understand the speaker's message is greatly hindered.

Moreover, noise pollution is a growing concern that affects our listening ability. Research has shown that exposure to excessive noise can lead to stress, fatigue, and cognitive impairment. This means that even if we are physically present in a conversation, our ability to truly comprehend and empathize with the speaker may be compromised due to the negative impact of noise on our cognitive functions.

To combat the challenges posed by environmental distractions and noise, it is crucial to create conducive listening environments. This can be achieved by finding quiet spaces where conversations can take place without interruptions from external stimuli. Additionally, it is important to set boundaries with technology, such as turning off notifications or putting phones on silent mode, to minimize distractions.

Furthermore, practicing active listening techniques can help us overcome the negative effects of environmental distractions. By focusing on the speaker, maintaining eye contact, and paraphrasing what they have said, we can ensure that we are fully present in the conversation and understand the speaker's message more effectively.

In conclusion, environmental distractions and noise pose significant challenges to our ability to be good listeners. However, by recognizing the impact of these distractions and implementing strategies to minimize their influence, we can enhance our listening skills and engage in more meaningful interactions. Ultimately, being a good listener requires creating a conducive environment that allows us to truly hear and understand others.

Techniques for minimizing external barriers

In order to become a good listener, it is essential to learn how to minimize external barriers that hinder effective communication. These external barriers can include environmental distractions, physical discomfort, and technological interruptions. By addressing and overcoming these obstacles, we can enhance our listening skills and create meaningful interactions.

One technique for minimizing external barriers is creating a conducive environment for listening. Find a quiet and comfortable space where you can focus your attention solely on the speaker. Turn off or silence any distracting devices such as phones or televisions. If possible, choose a location where interruptions are less likely to occur, allowing you to fully engage in the conversation.

Another technique is practicing active listening. This involves showing the speaker that you are fully present and engaged in the conversation. Maintain eye contact, nod to show understanding, and use verbal cues such as "I see", "uh-huh", or "go on" to encourage the speaker. By actively participating in the conversation, you not only minimize external distractions but also create an environment of trust and understanding.

Furthermore, it is important to be aware of and address any physical discomfort that may hinder your ability to listen effectively. Ensure that you are in a comfortable position, free from any pain or discomfort. If necessary, make adjustments to your seating or take short breaks to stretch and relax, allowing your body to be fully present and attentive.

Technological interruptions have become increasingly common in our modern world. To minimize their impact, it is crucial to set boundaries and establish rules when it comes to using electronic devices during conversations. Inform others of your intention to have a focused conversation and request that all devices be put on silent or turned off. By doing so, you create an environment that encourages uninterrupted communication.

In conclusion, by implementing techniques to minimize external barriers, we can enhance our listening skills and have more meaningful interactions. Creating a conducive environment, practicing active listening, addressing physical discomfort, and managing technological interruptions are all crucial steps towards becoming a good listener. By mastering these techniques, we can foster deeper connections, understanding, and empathy in our interactions with others.

Chapter 6: Listening for Personal and Professional Growth

The Role of Listening in Personal Development

In the fast-paced world we live in, where everyone seems to be in a rush to speak their mind, we often overlook the importance of being a good listener. Yet, listening is a powerful tool that can significantly impact our personal development. In this subchapter, we delve into the role of listening in personal growth and highlight the significance of being an attentive listener.

Listening is more than just hearing someone's words; it is about understanding their thoughts, emotions, and underlying messages. When we truly listen, we show respect and empathy towards others, fostering stronger relationships and connections. The act of listening allows us to gain valuable insights, broaden our perspectives, and learn from the experiences of others.

One of the key benefits of being a good listener is the impact it has on our personal growth. By actively listening to others, we open ourselves up to new ideas, knowledge, and wisdom. We become more receptive to feedback, enabling us to identify our strengths and weaknesses, and ultimately, improve ourselves. Through listening, we gain a deeper understanding of ourselves and the world around us, leading to personal growth and self-discovery.

Being a good listener also cultivates self-awareness. As we attentively listen to others, we become more attuned to our own thoughts, emotions, and biases. This heightened self-awareness allows us to identify and challenge our own limiting beliefs and assumptions, leading to personal breakthroughs and growth. By actively listening, we develop the ability to reflect on our own actions, thoughts, and behaviors, and make positive changes that align with our values and goals.

Moreover, listening plays a crucial role in developing effective communication skills. By listening attentively, we can truly understand others and respond in a meaningful way. This enhances our ability to express ourselves clearly and assertively, fostering better relationships and avoiding misunderstandings. The art of listening also helps us become more patient and empathetic, allowing us to connect with others on a deeper level and build stronger connections.

In conclusion, the importance of being a good listener cannot be overstated. It is a key ingredient in personal development, enabling us to gain valuable insights, foster self-awareness, and develop effective communication skills. By actively listening, we can unlock the hidden language of listening and discover the secrets to meaningful interactions. So, let us embrace the power of listening and embark on a journey of personal growth and connection with others.

Deepening self-awareness through listening

In today's fast-paced world, we often find ourselves engaged in countless conversations and interactions every day. But how often do we truly listen? Listening goes beyond just hearing words; it involves being fully present, understanding, and empathizing with the speaker. In this subchapter, we will explore the profound impact of deepening self-awareness through listening and understand why it is crucial for everyone.

Being a good listener is not only about showing respect to the speaker but also about gaining valuable insights into ourselves. When we truly listen, we open ourselves up to understanding our own thoughts, emotions, and beliefs. As we attentively listen to others, we inevitably reflect on our own experiences, biases, and perspectives. This process of self-reflection allows us to deepen our self-awareness, gaining a clearer understanding of who we are and how we relate to the world around us.

By actively listening, we become more attuned to our own values and beliefs. We begin to recognize patterns in our reactions and responses, enabling us to identify areas for personal growth and development. Deepening self-awareness through listening helps us uncover our strengths, weaknesses, and areas requiring improvement. It allows us to become more conscious of our triggers, biases, and assumptions, fostering personal growth and enhancing our relationships with others.

Moreover, listening helps us develop empathy and compassion. When we truly listen, we immerse ourselves in the speaker's world, trying to understand their perspective and experiences. This empathetic connection not only enhances our ability to communicate effectively but also enables us to build stronger relationships based on trust and understanding. Empathy is a fundamental skill that not only benefits our personal lives but also has a profound impact on our professional success.

In conclusion, deepening self-awareness through listening is a transformative process that benefits everyone. By being a good listener, we gain valuable insights into ourselves, allowing us to understand our own values, beliefs, and areas for personal growth. Additionally, listening helps us develop empathy and compassion, enhancing our relationships and fostering personal and professional success. So, let us embrace the hidden language of listening and unlock the secrets to meaningful interactions.

Strengthening personal relationships

In this subchapter, we delve into the importance of being a good listener in order to strengthen personal relationships. In today's fast-paced world, where distractions are abundant and time seems to be slipping away, meaningful interactions have become increasingly rare. However, mastering the art of listening can help us bridge this gap and foster deeper connections with our loved ones, friends, and even acquaintances.

Listening is a fundamental aspect of effective communication. It goes beyond simply hearing the words someone is saying and requires active engagement and empathy. When we truly listen, we show respect and genuine interest in the other person's thoughts, feelings, and experiences.

One of the key benefits of being a good listener is the ability to understand others on a deeper level. By paying attention to both verbal and non-verbal cues, we can gain insights into their emotions, needs, and desires. This understanding forms the foundation for stronger personal relationships, as it allows us to provide support, offer guidance, and celebrate their successes together.

Furthermore, listening allows us to validate and acknowledge the feelings of others. Oftentimes, people simply want to be heard and understood. By giving them our undivided attention, we create a safe space for them to express themselves without judgment. This validation can lead to a sense of trust and openness, which are vital for building and maintaining healthy relationships.

Being a good listener also means being present in the moment. In our fast-paced lives, it is easy to become preoccupied with our own thoughts and concerns. However, when we make a conscious effort to be fully present during conversations, we demonstrate our commitment and value for the relationship. By putting aside distractions and giving our undivided attention, we show that the other person's words and experiences matter to us.

Lastly, being a good listener enhances our own personal growth. When we actively listen to others, we expose ourselves to diverse perspectives and experiences. This not only broadens our understanding of the world but also helps us learn from others' wisdom and insights. By cultivating the habit of listening, we become more empathetic, compassionate, and understanding individuals.

In conclusion, strengthening personal relationships is crucial in today's society, and being a good listener is a key component of achieving this goal. By actively engaging with others, understanding their needs, validating their feelings, and being present in the moment, we can foster deeper connections and create a supportive network of individuals who truly understand and care for one another. So, let us embrace the hidden language of listening and embark on a journey towards meaningfully interacting with those around us.

The Impact of Listening in Professional Settings

In today's fast-paced world, where communication is key, being a good listener has become an indispensable skill in professional settings. Whether you are a manager, team leader, or simply a team member, the ability to listen effectively can have a profound impact on your career and the success of your organization. In this subchapter, we will explore the importance of being a good listener and the ways it can benefit you in professional settings.

Firstly, being a good listener promotes effective communication. When you actively listen to your colleagues, superiors, or clients, you create an environment where ideas can be freely shared, and conflicts can be resolved more easily. By truly understanding what others are saying, you can respond appropriately and contribute to productive discussions. This not only helps build strong relationships but also enhances teamwork and collaboration, which are vital for success in any professional setting.

Furthermore, being a good listener demonstrates respect and empathy towards others. By giving your full attention to someone, you show that you value their opinions and perspectives. This fosters trust and strengthens professional relationships, leading to better teamwork and increased productivity. Additionally, when you listen empathetically, you gain a deeper understanding of people's needs and concerns. This allows you to provide more effective support, whether it is in the form of guidance, problem-solving, or simply lending a listening ear.

Good listeners also possess a greater ability to learn and grow professionally. By actively listening to others' experiences and expertise, you can broaden your knowledge and gain valuable insights. This not only benefits your own personal development but also enables you to contribute more effectively to your team and organization. Moreover, being a good listener encourages open-mindedness and the exchange of ideas, which can lead to innovation and creative problem-solving.

Overall, the impact of listening in professional settings cannot be underestimated. It is a skill that has the power to transform the way we interact and collaborate with others, ultimately leading to greater success in our careers. By being a good listener, you can promote effective communication, build strong relationships, demonstrate respect and empathy, and enhance your ability to learn and grow. So, let us recognize the importance of listening and strive to become better listeners in our professional lives.

Improving teamwork and collaboration

In today's fast-paced world, effective teamwork and collaboration have become more critical than ever. In every facet of life, whether it is at work, in relationships, or within communities, the ability to work together harmoniously and achieve common goals is essential. This subchapter explores the significance of being a good listener in enhancing teamwork and collaboration.

The importance of being a good listener cannot be overstated. Listening is not merely the act of hearing words; it goes beyond that. It involves truly understanding and empathizing with others, which fosters a sense of trust and connection. By actively listening, we create an environment where collaboration can thrive.

One of the key ways to improve teamwork and collaboration is by cultivating a culture of open communication. When team members feel heard and valued, they are more likely to contribute their ideas and perspectives. By listening attentively, we encourage others to speak up, which leads to a diverse range of viewpoints and innovative solutions. This collaborative mindset creates a more inclusive and productive environment.

Additionally, being a good listener helps in resolving conflicts and diffusing tense situations. When conflicts arise, it is crucial to listen to all parties involved without judgment. By doing so, we can better understand the underlying issues and find common ground. Active listening enables us to validate emotions and facilitate a more constructive dialogue, leading to effective conflict resolution and strengthened relationships.

Furthermore, teamwork and collaboration heavily rely on effective teamwork and collaboration heavily rely on effective communication. Being a good listener allows us to grasp the nuances of verbal and non-verbal cues, enabling us to respond appropriately. By listening carefully, we avoid misunderstandings and confusion, leading to smoother teamwork and improved outcomes.

In conclusion, improving teamwork and collaboration requires us to embrace the role of a good listener. By actively listening and valuing the perspectives of others, we create a culture of open communication, trust, and inclusivity. This, in turn, leads to enhanced problem-solving, conflict resolution, and overall productivity. Whether in our personal or professional lives, being a good listener is a powerful tool that fosters meaningful interactions and enables us to achieve success together.

Enhancing leadership and decision-making skills

Effective leadership and decision-making skills are essential in today's fast-paced and dynamic world. In the book "The Hidden Language of Listening: Discovering the Secrets to Meaningful Interactions," we delve into the importance of being a good listener and how it can significantly enhance your leadership capabilities and decision-making prowess.

Listening is often overlooked as a crucial aspect of effective leadership. However, it is a skill that can make a world of difference in how you connect with others, inspire your team, and make informed decisions. By actively listening to others, you gain valuable insights, foster trust, and build strong relationships – all of which are fundamental to effective leadership.

Being a good listener enables you to understand the needs, desires, and concerns of your team members, stakeholders, and customers. It allows you to gather diverse perspectives, which can lead to more well-rounded decisions. By truly listening, you create an environment where people feel heard and valued, encouraging collaboration, creativity, and innovation.

Furthermore, listening helps you develop empathy, a crucial trait for effective leadership. When you genuinely listen, you demonstrate that you care about others' thoughts and feelings, fostering a culture of inclusivity and respect. This, in turn, enhances your ability to motivate and inspire others, ultimately leading to better team performance.

In the realm of decision-making, listening plays a critical role. By actively listening to different viewpoints, you gain a deeper understanding of complex situations and can make more informed choices. It helps you identify potential pitfalls, consider alternative solutions, and evaluate the impact of your decisions on various stakeholders.

In "The Hidden Language of Listening," you will discover practical strategies and techniques to enhance your listening skills, ultimately improving your leadership abilities and decision-making processes. You will learn how to cultivate mindful listening habits, ask powerful questions, and leverage active listening techniques to create meaningful interactions with those around you.

Whether you are a seasoned leader, aspiring manager, or simply someone looking to enhance their interpersonal skills, this subchapter will provide you with invaluable insights into the importance of being a good listener. By honing your listening skills, you can elevate your leadership abilities, build stronger relationships, and make better decisions, ultimately leading to success in both your personal and professional endeavors.

Chapter 7: Cultivating the Habit of Listening

Practicing Mindful Listening

In today's fast-paced world, where distractions are constantly vying for our attention, the art of truly listening seems to be fading away. However, being a good listener is not just a skill, but an essential quality that can greatly enhance our personal and professional relationships. By practicing mindful listening, we can unlock the secrets to meaningful interactions and experience the true power of understanding.

The importance of being a good listener cannot be overstated. When we listen mindfully, we create a safe and supportive space for others to express themselves. This fosters trust and deepens our connections with loved ones, colleagues, and even strangers. Mindful listening allows us to truly hear and understand others, validating their thoughts, feelings, and experiences. It helps us to suspend judgment, setting aside our own biases and preconceptions, and immersing ourselves in the present moment.

Beyond the benefits to our relationships, mindful listening also enriches our own lives. By giving our full attention to the speaker, we open ourselves up to new perspectives and insights. We learn from others, broadening our understanding of the world around us. Mindful listening encourages empathy and compassion, enabling us to support others during challenging times. It also helps us become more self-aware, as we become attuned to our own thoughts, emotions, and reactions while listening.

Practicing mindful listening requires intention and discipline. It begins with cultivating a mindset of curiosity and genuine interest in what others have to say. We must be fully present, setting aside distractions and giving our undivided attention. Active listening techniques, such as maintaining eye contact, using open body language, and offering verbal and non-verbal cues, can further enhance our ability to connect with others.

It is important to remember that mindful listening is a continuous practice. It requires patience, as well as a willingness to challenge our own assumptions and beliefs. By embracing the hidden language of listening, we can transform our relationships and create a more harmonious world. So, let us embark on this journey together and discover the secrets to meaningful interactions through the power of mindful listening.

Techniques for being fully present in conversations

In our fast-paced world filled with distractions, it can be challenging to truly engage in meaningful conversations. However, being fully present in conversations is crucial for establishing deep connections, fostering understanding, and building strong relationships. In this subchapter, we will explore some effective techniques that can help anyone become a better listener and be fully present in conversations.

1. Cultivate Mindfulness: Mindfulness is the practice of being fully aware and present in the current moment. By training ourselves to be mindful, we can significantly enhance our listening skills. Practice focusing your attention on the person speaking, letting go of any distractions or preconceived notions. Engage all your senses and take in the speaker's words, tone, and body language.

2. Active Listening: Active listening involves not only hearing the words being spoken but also understanding the underlying message and emotions. Pay attention to the speaker's non-verbal cues, such as facial expressions and gestures. Show your engagement by nodding, maintaining eye contact, and providing verbal cues like "I see," "I understand," or asking thoughtful questions.

3. Avoid Interrupting: Interrupting someone not only disrupts the flow of conversation but also indicates a lack of respect for the speaker. Practice patience and allow the speaker to finish their thoughts before contributing your own. This shows that you value their opinion and are genuinely interested in what they have to say.

4. Practice Empathy: Empathy is the ability to understand and share the feelings of another person. Put yourself in the speaker's shoes and

try to grasp their perspective. Validate their emotions and respond with empathy, showing that you genuinely care about their experiences.

5. Minimize Distractions: In today's digital age, it is easy to get distracted by our phones, notifications, or other external stimuli. To be fully present in conversations, eliminate distractions by putting your phone on silent or in another room. Create a conducive environment that allows you to focus solely on the person in front of you.

6. Reflect and Summarize: After the speaker has finished expressing their thoughts, take a moment to reflect on what they said. Summarize their main points to ensure you have understood correctly. This not only reinforces your understanding but also shows the speaker that you were actively listening.

By employing these techniques, you can become a better listener and fully engage in conversations. Remember, being fully present in conversations not only benefits you but also the speaker. It fosters trust, respect, and meaningful interactions, leading to stronger relationships and a deeper understanding of others. So, let us strive to be fully present in our conversations and unlock the hidden language of listening.

Incorporating listening into daily routines

Listening is an art that has the power to transform our daily interactions and relationships. It is a skill that can be honed and practiced, and when done effectively, it can create meaningful connections with others. In this subchapter, we will explore the importance of incorporating listening into our daily routines, and how it can positively impact our lives.

First and foremost, being a good listener is crucial in building strong and healthy relationships. Whether it is with our family, friends, colleagues, or even strangers, actively listening to others shows that we value and respect their thoughts and feelings. By incorporating listening into our daily routines, we can foster deeper connections with those around us, leading to more fulfilling and meaningful interactions.

One way to incorporate listening into our daily routines is by setting aside dedicated time for meaningful conversations. In our fast-paced and busy lives, it is easy to get caught up in our own thoughts and agendas. However, by carving out specific moments in our day to engage in genuine conversations, we can create space for active listening. This could be during meal times, coffee breaks, or even during a daily walk. By giving our undivided attention to the speaker, we can truly listen and understand their perspective, fostering empathy and strengthening our relationships.

Another way to incorporate listening into our daily routines is by practicing mindfulness. Mindfulness is the practice of being fully present in the moment, without judgment. By cultivating mindfulness, we can become more attuned to the needs and emotions of others. This allows us to listen with intention and respond in a more empathetic and supportive manner. Incorporating mindfulness practices, such as meditation or deep breathing exercises, into our daily routines can enhance our listening skills and improve our overall well-being.

Furthermore, technology plays a significant role in our daily lives, often distracting us from being fully present. To incorporate listening into our routines, it is essential to minimize distractions. This means putting away electronic devices, turning off notifications, and creating a quiet and peaceful environment. By eliminating distractions, we can focus on the speaker's words and nonverbal cues, enhancing our ability to listen effectively.

In conclusion, incorporating listening into our daily routines is crucial for developing meaningful interactions and relationships. By setting aside dedicated time for conversations, practicing mindfulness, and minimizing distractions, we can become better listeners. The art of listening is a powerful tool that can transform our lives, allowing us to connect with others on a deeper level and create more fulfilling relationships. So, let us make a conscious effort to incorporate listening into our daily routines and discover the hidden language of listening.

The Journey of Becoming a Better Listener

In today's fast-paced world, where distractions are abundant and attention spans are shrinking, the art of listening has become a lost skill. Yet, being a good listener is more important than ever before. It is a skill that can transform our personal and professional relationships, leading to more meaningful interactions and connections. This subchapter explores the journey of becoming a better listener and highlights the importance of cultivating this skill in our lives.

Being a good listener is not a passive act; it is an active process that requires intention and practice. It involves giving our complete attention to the person speaking, suspending judgment, and empathizing with their thoughts and emotions. By truly listening, we can understand others' perspectives, needs, and desires, fostering deeper connections and building trust.

The journey of becoming a better listener starts with self-awareness. We must recognize our own listening habits and identify areas where we can improve. Are we often distracted by our phones or preoccupied with our own thoughts during conversations? Acknowledging these tendencies allows us to make a conscious effort to be present and attentive.

Next, we must cultivate empathy. Empathy is the ability to understand and share the feelings of another person. By putting ourselves in someone else's shoes, we can grasp their emotions and experiences more fully. This enables us to respond with compassion and support, creating a safe space for open and honest communication.

Additionally, active listening involves asking thoughtful questions and providing feedback. These actions show genuine interest in the speaker and encourage them to share more deeply. By asking open-ended questions, we invite them to explore their thoughts and feelings, leading to richer and more meaningful conversations.

Furthermore, becoming a better listener requires patience and practice. It is a skill that develops over time with consistent effort. We must be willing to commit ourselves to the process and be patient with ourselves as we navigate the challenges and setbacks along the way.

In conclusion, the journey of becoming a better listener is a transformative one. It involves self-awareness, empathy, active engagement, and patience. By honing this skill, we can enhance our relationships, deepen our understanding of others, and foster more meaningful interactions. So, let us embark on this journey together, for the rewards of being a good listener are immeasurable.

Setting goals and tracking progress

In the journey towards becoming a good listener, setting goals and tracking progress is of utmost importance. It is through this process that we can truly discover the secrets to meaningful interactions. Whether you are a student, a professional, a parent, or simply someone who wants to enhance their communication skills, this chapter will guide you in understanding the significance of setting goals and tracking your progress.

Goal setting acts as a compass, providing direction and focus in our pursuit of becoming better listeners. By setting specific, measurable, achievable, relevant, and time-bound (SMART) goals, we can systematically work towards improving our listening skills. For instance, you may set a goal to actively listen during a conversation with a friend or colleague for ten minutes without interrupting or judging. Another goal may involve practicing empathetic listening by putting yourself in the other person's shoes and understanding their perspective. The key is to set goals that challenge you while being realistic and attainable.

Once goals are set, it is crucial to track your progress. This allows you to assess how far you have come and identify areas that require further improvement. Tracking progress can be done through self-reflection, journaling, or seeking feedback from others. Reflect on your listening experiences and evaluate whether you met your goals. Did you listen attentively? Were you able to understand the underlying emotions? Did you provide meaningful responses? Journaling can be a powerful tool to record your thoughts, observations, and experiences, enabling you to identify patterns and areas for growth.

Seeking feedback from others is equally important. Engage in open and honest conversations with trusted friends, family members, or colleagues who can provide constructive criticism. They may have noticed changes in your listening skills or have suggestions for further enhancement. Embrace their feedback with an open mind and use it as a stepping stone towards improvement.

Remember, the journey towards becoming a good listener is a continuous process. Setting goals and tracking progress ensures that you are constantly evolving and growing in your ability to connect with others. As you achieve your goals, celebrate your successes and set new ones that challenge you further. With each milestone, you will witness the transformation in your interactions, leading to more meaningful and fulfilling relationships.

So, take a moment to reflect on your listening skills, set SMART goals, and embark on this journey of self-discovery and growth. The rewards of becoming a better listener are immense, and the impact it can have on your personal and professional life is immeasurable. Start today and unlock the hidden language of listening.

Seeking feedback and continuous improvement

In the journey of becoming a good listener, seeking feedback and continuous improvement play a crucial role. Listening is an art that requires constant honing and refining, and incorporating feedback is essential to enhance our skills. This subchapter will delve into the significance of seeking feedback and the ways in which continuous improvement can shape us into better listeners.

Feedback is a powerful tool that allows us to gain valuable insights into our listening abilities. By actively seeking feedback from others, we open ourselves up to constructive criticism and guidance that can propel our listening skills forward. Whether it's from friends, family, colleagues, or even strangers, feedback provides us with a fresh perspective and helps us identify areas for improvement. It allows us to understand how others perceive our listening skills and offers an opportunity for growth.

Furthermore, seeking feedback fosters a culture of open communication and trust. When we actively seek feedback, we demonstrate our commitment to self-improvement and our willingness to learn from others. This encourages honest and open conversations, paving the way for more meaningful interactions. By welcoming feedback, we create an environment where others feel comfortable sharing their thoughts and experiences, leading to deeper connections and enhanced understanding.

Continuous improvement is closely tied to seeking feedback. It involves a commitment to consistently refining our listening skills and incorporating feedback into our practice. It requires a growth mindset and a genuine desire to become a better listener. Continuous improvement involves actively seeking out resources, such as books, articles, workshops, or even coaching, to expand our knowledge and understanding of effective listening techniques.

Moreover, continuous improvement necessitates self-reflection. Taking the time to reflect on our listening experiences allows us to identify patterns, strengths, and areas that require improvement. Through self-reflection, we gain insights into our listening habits, biases, and distractions. This self-awareness empowers us to address these challenges and adapt our approach accordingly.

In conclusion, seeking feedback and continuous improvement are fundamental aspects of becoming a good listener. By actively seeking feedback, we gain valuable insights and open ourselves up to growth opportunities. Continuous improvement, on the other hand, involves a commitment to refining our skills through self-reflection and the incorporation of feedback. Together, these practices contribute to the development of meaningful interactions and foster stronger connections with others. Embrace the power of feedback and the journey of continuous improvement to unlock the hidden language of listening.

Conclusion: Unleashing the Power of Listening in Your Life

In today's fast-paced world, where communication has become increasingly digital and instantaneous, the art of listening has taken a backseat. However, being a good listener is more important than ever before. It not only helps us forge deeper connections with others but also allows us to gain a deeper understanding of ourselves. In this concluding chapter, we will explore the importance of being a good listener and how it can positively impact various aspects of our lives.

Listening is a skill that transcends boundaries and applies to everyone. Whether you are a student, a professional, a parent, or a friend, the ability to truly listen can transform your relationships and enhance your personal growth. By actively listening, we show respect and empathy, creating an environment that encourages open and honest communication. This, in turn, fosters trust and strengthens the bonds we share with others.

In our professional lives, being a good listener can make all the difference. It allows us to understand clients' needs, collaborate effectively with colleagues, and lead teams to success. By listening attentively, we can identify opportunities, solve problems, and make informed decisions. Moreover, being a good listener can significantly improve our communication skills, making us more persuasive and influential in our interactions.

On a personal level, being a good listener can greatly enhance our relationships. It shows our loved ones that we value their thoughts and feelings, creating a sense of validation and security. By listening, we can provide support and comfort during challenging times, strengthening our connections and deepening our understanding of one another. Furthermore, being a good listener allows us to learn from others' experiences and broaden our perspectives, enriching our own lives in the process.

To become a better listener, we must cultivate a mindset of curiosity and openness. We need to set aside our own agendas and truly focus on what the other person is saying. This means actively engaging with them through eye contact, body language, and verbal cues. We should also practice empathy, trying to understand their emotions and see the world from their perspective. By doing so, we can create a safe and non-judgmental space for meaningful interactions to occur.

In conclusion, being a good listener is a powerful tool that can transform our lives in numerous ways. It allows us to connect deeply with others, foster trust, and create meaningful relationships. It enhances our professional success by improving communication and decision-making skills. Most importantly, being a good listener enables us to learn and grow, opening doors to new perspectives and enriching our personal development. So, let us embrace the hidden language of listening and unleash its power in our lives.

Printed in the USA
CPSIA information can be obtained
at www.ICGtesting.com
CBHW050525040824
12618CB00051B/700